MW00509706

SPOTIFY:
MUSIC FOR EVERYONE

The meteoric rise of the world's top
streaming service

Written by Charlotte Bouillot
Translated by Emma Hanna

Business **50MINUTES**.com

50MINUTES.com

PROPEL
YOUR BUSINESS FORWARD!

Blue Ocean Strategy

Pareto's Principle

Managing Stress at Work

Game Theory

www.50minutes.com

SPOTIFY: MUSIC FOR EVERYONE

Key information

- **Founders:** Daniel Ek (Swedish entrepreneur, born in 1983) and Martin Lorentzon (Swedish engineer, born in 1969).
- **Founded:** Spotify was originally founded in Sweden in 2006 and has been available to the public since 7 October 2008 (when it was launched in Sweden, Great Britain, France, Spain, Finland and Norway).
- **Sector:** entertainment, music and video.
- **Marketing area:** as of 2017, Spotify is now available in over 60 countries worldwide, having launched in the United States in 2011 and in Latin America and parts of Asia in 2013.
- **Number of users:** as of October 2017, Spotify has over 140 million active users, of whom over 60 million (i.e. 42%) are

paying subscribers.

- **Annual turnover:** over $3.3 billion in 2016, compared with $2.18 billion in 2015, with subscriptions accounting for around 90% of revenue and advertising accounting for the remaining 10%.
- **Key terms:**
  - **Freemium:** this portmanteau of the words "free" and "premium" was first used by the American investor and blogger Fred Wilson in 2006. It denotes a commercial service which offers both a basic version which is free to access and use, and a "premium" version which offers more advanced features to paying users. The free version is often financed by advertisements and can attract users who are eventually persuaded to sign up for the paid version.
  - **Premium:** a premium service is an enhanced version of the basic service offered by a service provider using a "freemium" business model. The premium service is usually significantly more expensive. On Spotify, the bonus features offered by the Premium service

include higher sound quality, the option of using the service offline, and the removal of all adverts.

○ **Royalties:** royalties are the payment owed to a creator in exchange for the right to use their work, patent or brand. They are a means of complying with co-pyright law, which recognises creators as the only individuals with the right to distribute their work until it enters the public domain.

Spotify has been hailed as revolutionary because of the way it has shaken up the music industry, causing no shortage of debate in the process. While it used to be impossible to listen to a music file without buying it, streaming technology is now sufficiently advanced to allow audio files to be played without being downloaded. As the file is not being downloaded, there is no need to pay for it, although this business model of paid downloads is still used by iTunes, Apple's music player software, among others.

Unlike many of Spotify's competitors, such as Google, Apple and Amazon, the company was not founded in the US, and it was only launched there three years after its initial European launch in 2008. However, the phenomenon soon gained momentum on the other side of the Atlantic: the number of songs streamed online by users in the United States increased by a whopping 50% between 2013 and 2014, while the volume of paid downloads dropped by 13% in the same period. Today, Spotify is the most-downloaded app in the United States.

There is only one fly in the ointment, but it is a big one – certain artists feel that their share of the profits is unacceptably slim, and have rebelled against the site. According to a report published in December 2013 by ADAMI, a French organisation which oversees the rights of artists and musicians, streamed songs can generate as much as 22 times more revenue than the royalties received by the artists.

At a time when the music industry is waging war on streaming, and when competition within the sector is constantly getting fiercer, how do the creators of this phenomenally popular service envisage its future?

THE EARLY DAYS

THE ENTREPRENEUR AND THE VISIONARY

Daniel Ek is a Swedish computer programmer who was born in Stockholm in 1983. By the age of 14, he had already become a CEO, coding and hosting professional websites from his bedroom. When he was only 16 years old, he began wondering how the public could be persuaded to pay for music that could be downloaded for free (albeit illegally). In 2005, he abandoned his engineering studies at the KTH Royal Institute of Technology in Sweden to begin a career in online marketing, and founded Advertigo.

Martin Lorentzon was born in 1969. He is a Swedish businessman who studied for an MBA in Gothenburg before embarking on a career which saw him sitting on the board of directors of several large companies such as Telia and Cell Ventures. In 1999, he founded Tradedoubler, which went on to become Europe's largest affiliate network.

Affiliation, whereby a website hosts advertising on behalf of a third party who pays a fee to the owner of the site, is commonplace nowadays, but at that time it was a revolutionary concept, as Amazon had only just started using it in the United States, and Google still had not even started using targeted advertising.

In 2006, Ek sold Advertigo to Tradedoubler, and the two men joined forces to create the world's largest online music player: Spotify.

THE DIGITAL REVOLUTION

On 11 November 2014, Ek made a post on the official Spotify blog in which he reminded users of the site's origins.

> "We started Spotify because we love music and piracy was killing it." (Ek 2011)

Since Napster – a peer-to-peer (P2P) file-sharing service, which means that each user also acts as a server so that files can be directly transmitted from one computer to another without passing through a central server – appeared in 1999, music sales have fallen considerably and the future looks no brighter. According to the IFPI, the organisation which ensures that copyright is enforced in the music industry, the industry's sales volume fell by 23% and its sales value fell by 16% worldwide between 1999 and 2003 alone.

Peer-to-peer (P2P) software

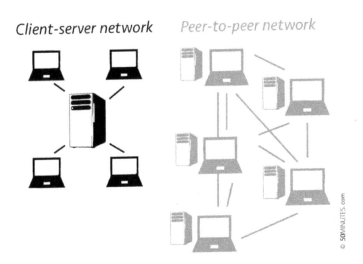

This model was later adopted by many different file-sharing platforms, including Spotify.

MUSIC SALES CERTIFICATIONS

The sales thresholds that albums must reach to be certified silver, gold, platinum or diamond have had to be lowered on a regular basis since their inception due to the changing market. For example, the RIAA, which oversees music sales certification in the USA, currently awards a Platinum certification when a single sells 1 million units, but the Platinum certification was originally reserved for singles which had sold a minimum of 2 million units.

MUSIC FOR EVERYONE

In the same way that the emergence of commercial radio broadcasting rocked the record industry in the 1930s, recent developments in digital technology have led to new consumer habits.

Practically unlimited music access

Any internet user can now access a near-infinite range of music (over 30 million songs are available on Spotify as of October 2017) without having to spend a penny. This means they are able to flick between genres, artists and albums at their leisure, while also discovering new talent. Even though these users are probably buying fewer CDs or downloadable files, they are nevertheless consuming much more music.

RECORD-BREAKING LISTENING HABITS

In February 2001, when Napster was at its zenith, 2.79 billion songs were downloaded via the site. Meanwhile, the equivalent of one million years' worth of music was listened to via Spotify in just the first five years of the site's existence!

These two giants share a common goal: to provide the most complete, high-quality range of music possible in order to satisfy their users' insatiable appetite for music.

Music is everywhere

Music occupies an increasingly important place in our daily lives. Since 2000, when compressing audio files in MP3 format became common, music has become a digitalised commodity and can be played on all kinds of online and offline devices, anywhere and at any time. Music has become indispensable: it provides individuals with a way of finding their identity while allowing groups of people to find common ground. While digitalisation may have significantly reduced the price that consumers are willing to pay for songs, the value that listeners place on their music has never been higher.

An experience to be shared

Thanks to digitalisation, consumers are no longer interested in the end product alone, but also in the experience that comes with it: discovering a song, listening to it, sharing it on social media, making contact with other fans, meeting the artist and their followers at concerts and festivals – which are, in fact, seeing increased attendance rates.

By streaming live concerts, providing access to playlists, interviews with celebrities and unreleased music, and holding raffles for concert tickets, Spotify makes music a more social experience than ever before, which doubtlessly contributes to its colossal success.

Similarly, the platform is ultra-connected to social media, and provides developers with the necessary tools to integrate its catalogue and features in new apps, on new websites, and even in new programmes. One example is the app Roadtrip Mixtape, which uses Spotify to create playlists featuring local artists based on your planned route.

In so doing, Spotify:

- sends a strong message: "there is no need to reinvent the wheel, Spotify has done it for you!";
- is aiming for a lofty goal: to be at the centre of new developments and constantly increase its user base.

> "Our whole reason for existence is to help fans find music and help artists connect with fans through a platform that protects them from piracy and pays them for their amazing work." (Ek 2014)

SPOTIFY'S EVOLUTION

HOW IS SPOTIFY FUNDED?

The early investors

The project was born when a pair of entrepreneurs decided to work together by combining their two shared passions: music and technology. Their dream was to create the world's largest online music player by combining the peer-to-peer software model with a business model financed by advertisements. The original prototype was inspired by the iTunes user interface set against an elegant black background reminiscent of a flat-screen television.

Ek and Lorentzon initially financed the project out of their own pockets: the former was a young IT expert who had become a self-made millionaire by the age of 23 thanks to a programme he had developed for Tradedoubler, while the latter had earned $70 million by putting Tradedoubler on the stock market in 2005.

Although Ek had thought that they would be able to obtain the necessary music licences within a few months, it actually took two years. The music industry was extremely reluctant to experiment with this new model, which was at that time completely untested, and the record labels demanded huge advance payments before leasing out their catalogues. Despite the huge investments that they had already made when launching the business, the two entrepreneurs soon had to inject nearly $5 million in additional funding into their endeavour.

However, it was not long before the project attracted additional investors, including some of the big names in social network development: Sean Parker, the co-founder of Napster and the former president of Facebook, and his investment fund Founders Fund; Li Ka-Shing, a Hong Kong businessman who had invested $60 million in Facebook in 2007; and the Russian investment fund Digital Sky Technologies, which had already funded Facebook, Groupon, Twitter, and Airbnb.

The freemium business model

Spotify is a programme linked to a website which allows users to stream music through a peer-to-peer server model. In practice, users can choose between two services:

- the free but limited service (funded by advertisements);
- the unlimited Premium service, which is available by paid subscription only.

This is known as a freemium model, which is very common in video games and social networks.

Freemium

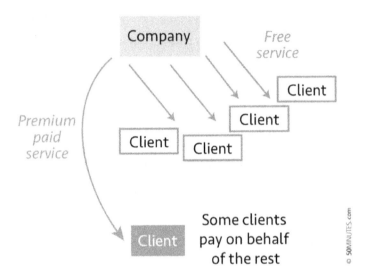

According to Ek, this two-service model is what enables Spotify to attract users who were previously used to illegally downloading music for free.

METEORIC SUCCESS

Spotify was launched on 7 October 2008 and attracted 7 million users in Europe in less than two years, of whom 250 000 subscribed to the Premium service. The site reached one million subscribers in March 2011, attesting to its tremendous success. That same year, Spotify cemented its position as a market leader by signing a deal with Warner Music, kicking off the streaming revolution in the United States.

The best platform on the planet

Ek's goals are ambitious: "We are hyper-focused on creating the best user experience and it starts with building the best music intelligence platform on the planet." To achieve that goal, the company is constantly tweaking its services and adds new features almost monthly.

- **October 2013:** Spotify launched Spotify Connect, which allows users to play music over wireless speakers, using the Spotify mobile app as a remote control.
- **December 2013:** the Spotify TV app was launched for LG Smart TVs in over 30 countries, and the free Spotify app became available across all iOS and Android devices.
- **March 2014:** Spotify took one step closer to becoming the world's number one search en-

gine for music with the acquisition of The Echo Nest, an intelligent music platform which analyses listener behaviour to help suggest other songs for them.

- **May 2014:** Spotify formed a partnership with djay, the most popular DJ app in the world, meaning that Premium djay users can now access the Spotify catalogue and its 30 million songs when mixing, and the app can now suggest song sequences.
- **November 2014:** Spotify signed a deal with Uber, an American company which puts the users of its mobile app in contact with private drivers as an alternative to taxis. This partnership allows users to select a Spotify playlist to be played during their Uber ride.
- **December 2014:** Spotify revealed the most popular albums, songs, artists and styles of the year, and created a personalised overview of each user's year in music (their most-listened genres, favourite artist each season, special moments, etc.).
- **February 2015:** Musixmatch, the world's largest catalogue of song lyrics, was integrated into the Spotify app, making it even easier for users to sing along to their favourite songs.

- **March 2015:** Spotify became an affiliate of Sony Computer Entertainment to create Playstation Music, thus allowing gamers to create their own soundtracks for their video games, to gain access to exclusive playlists, and to listen to their favourite albums directly from their TV screens.
- **May 2015:** Spotify began preparing to enter the video streaming market, which is significantly more profitable than the music market. In a press conference, Spotify announced that it had made deals with several content providers so that shows and series could be streamed on Spotify in their original form.
- **July 2015:** Spotify launched Discover Weekly, a playlist which is generated each week and provides users with two hours of customised music recommendations, mixing their personal taste with songs enjoyed by similar listeners.
- **January 2016:** Spotify formed a partnership with Genius, a music annotation service, so that annotation information from Genius can be displayed as info cards which appear while songs are playing in Spotify.
- **August 2016:** Spotify launched Release Radar, a personalised playlist that alerts users to new

music released by the artists they listen to most often.

- **September 2016:** Spotify introduced Daily Mix, a series of playlists that have "near endless playback" and mix the user's favourite tracks with new, recommended songs. New users can access Daily Mix after approximately two weeks of listening to music through Spotify.
- **May 2017:** Spotify introduced Spotify Codes for its mobile apps, a feature which allows users to share specific artists, tracks, playlists or albums with other people. Users can now generate barcodes which are unique to each piece of content, while an update to the Spotify app now allows users to access their device's camera via the app, which can then scan the codes generated by other listeners and take the user to that exact content.

COPYRIGHT

A free, legal catalogue of music

By creating a legal way to listen to music for free, Spotify made it possible to listen to tremendous quantities of music anywhere and at any time – a possibility that soon became an addiction for many users. Once music lovers get into the habit of listening to Spotify, their allegiance tends to shift irreversibly away from paid downloads and CDs, as these traditional sources of music are too expensive to be a sustainable way for listeners who have become accustomed to limitless streaming to quench their tremendous thirst for music. This was why Warner Music categorically refused to allow its catalogue to be added to Spotify until 2011, as the company had grave concerns over the possible long-term consequences for the CD industry.

It took the Swedish entrepreneurs two long years of negotiations with the four giants of the music industry (Sony Music, EMI, Universal Music and Warner Music) before Spotify was able to launch in the United States. In the end, significant concessions had to be made regarding the terms and conditions of Spotify's Free service. From then on, users could only listen to Spotify music for ten hours per month, and could only listen to each song a maximum of five times, unless they opted to pay for the Premium service. Pascal Nègre, the head of Universal Music France, made his views on the matter very clear in early 2011:

"When you see people listening to the same song 35 times, you say to yourself, at some point this guy has got to go and buy the song [...] If you listen to a song four times, that's enough to know whether or not you want to buy it."[1] (Nègre 2011)

These restrictions on Spotify's Free service were eventually lifted a year later – i.e. in 2012 – in most European countries, though they remained in place until June 2013 in France. Like Daniel Ek, Axel Dauchez, the former CEO of Deezer, one of Spotify's competitors, is convinced that offering a free service is the key to converting internet users to a paid system, and therefore condemned the idea of placing limitations on listener access as "counter-productive" in the French newspaper *Le Monde* in 2011.

DID YOU KNOW?

Although the Free service is an indispensable way for artists to increase their visibility and to reach new audiences worldwide, in 2013 Spotify revealed that 4 million of

---

1. This quotation has been translated by 50Minutes.com.

the songs it hosts – in other words, 20% of its catalogue at the time – had never been listened to. Even for well-known artists, the argument that they are being "discovered" is only true to a certain extent, as listeners often prefer to listen to one hit on a loop rather than taking an interest in an artist's entire discography. Because of this, certain groups lose the interest of up to 80% of listeners between the first and last track of an album (Perelstein 2013).

Shared value

At the end of 2014, the American star Taylor Swift released her fifth album, *1989*, but refused to make it available on Spotify, breathing new life into the old debate over remuneration for artists. Not long after being named "the best-paid woman in the music industry" by *Fortune* magazine and being the highest-ranked woman on its greatest leaders list, Swift also had all of her music removed from Spotify, asserting that the platform did not adequately compensate artists. Other artists have voiced similar views, including the British rock stars Thom Yorke (from

Radiohead) and Nigel Godrich (from Atoms for Peace).

Ek held firm in the face of these attacks, never wavering from his original position: that streaming is an inexpensive alternative to allowing piracy to go unchecked, and that the constantly growing number of users who opt to pay for Spotify's streaming service means that Spotify has paid artists more in royalties than certain radio stations, as well as most of its competitors. In fact, between the company's creation in 2008 and November 2014, when Ek made his case via a post on the Spotify blog, Spotify had paid over $2 billion to the music industry, or the equivalent of 70% of its revenue. However, this argument raises other questions: how much money is earned through streaming, and who benefits from royalties?

Copyright in France

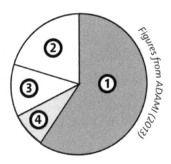

Figures from ADAMI (2013)

① **€6.54**
*to intermediaries - 70% to producers,
30% to streaming platforms*

② **€1.99**
to the government (VAT)

③ **€1**
to the copyright holder

④ **€0.46**
*to the artists (divided by all songs listened
to in a month)*

ADAMI, the organisation in charge of overseeing
music copyright in France, published a report in
December 2013 regarding the value distribution
of online music. This report highlighted the imba-
lanced way that revenue from online streaming

is shared out: of the €9.99 that Spotify Premium users pay each month in Western Europe, €6.54 goes to intermediaries (€4.58 to the producers and €1.96 to Spotify), €1.99 goes to the government (VAT), €1 goes to the copyright holder (songwriters) and €0.46 to the artists (given that songs are not necessarily written and sung by the same person).

Based on figures from 2013 (4.7 billion hours of listening by 30 million users of both the Free and Premium services), an average listener can be assumed to consume around 260 songs which are each approximately three minutes in length each month on Spotify. There is no need to divide the amount earned by the artists (€1.46) by 260 to make it clear that this model does not provide significant benefits for creators. While paid downloads had already led to artists being paid less per album sold (€0.43 per album sold online compared to €0.75 per CD sold), streaming has sent their wages into total freefall. Yet if it were not for the songwriters, composers and singers of the world, Spotify would not exist. A few years ago, 130 organisations representing over 500 000 European artists joined forces to create the Fair Internet For Performers movement, which campaigns for internet sales to compensate artists fairly.

Artists' share of CD sales

	Physical disk	Digital download
Under 50 000 albums sold	6.40%	5.10%
Between 50 000 and 200 000 albums sold	8.10%	6.40%
More than 200 000 albums sold	9.70%	7.70%

Average artists' share per single sold/ streamed online

Single sold on iTunes	Song streamed for free	Song streamed by a paid subscriber
€0.04	€0.0001	€0.004

IMPACT

A VIABLE BUSINESS MODEL?

As of October 2017, Spotify has over 60 million subscribers in 61 countries worldwide, a strong presence on the American market and an approach which is strongly oriented towards social media, making the platform practically ubiquitous across the internet. However, the figures paint a bleaker picture.

Although the company brought in over $3.3 billion in turnover in 2017, this only represented an annual increase of 52%, compared to an increase of 80% in 2015 and an increase of 128% in 2012. Worst of all, its net loss grew to an eye-watering $597 million. This raises the question of whether or not this economic model will actually prove to be profitable in the long term. Similarly, the company's main rival Deezer enjoyed a short period of profitability in 2011 before plunging back into the red. Given that Spotify has always paid 70% of all its profits to copyright holders (artists and intermediaries) in royalties, the company will undoubtedly struggle to increase its margins, even with higher revenues. According to analysts, the company's estimated value of $13 billion (as of May 2017, according to *Reuters*) could represent another stumbling block by deterring larger companies from acquiring it.

2014: MARKET FRAGMENTATION

The world of audio streaming was a two-horse race between Spotify and the French start-up Deezer for several years. However, the market was shaken up in 2014, which saw the streaming phenomenon really take hold in the United States, the legal download market start to flounder, and several new players enter the frantic race to monopolise on-demand music.

Market fragmentation

Spotify
N° 1
the market leader,
with 60 million
subscribers - but still
is not turning
a profit

Deezer
N° 2
6 million subscribers
in 180 countries.
The largest
catalogue at 40
million songs

Apple
gets back in the race

Amazon
launches a streaming service
(for music and books)

Google
and Youtube Music Key

Qobuz
with an HD catalogue
(more expensive)

Heavyweight competitors muscling in

Apple's empire was originally built on music downloads (iPod, iTunes, etc.), a market which was falling into a slump. However, the firm burst back onto the scene in style by purchasing Beats by Dr Dre, a company which sells audio headphones and provides a streaming service, for $3 billion. Beats headphones are now sold under the Apple umbrella, and the streaming service Beats Music was integrated into a rebranded service known as Apple Music in 2015. Apple's marketing strategy is based on automatically suggesting its own streaming service on Apple tablets and smartphones so that users can access it at any time, meaning that those who have already signed up to another streaming platform may be enticed to jump ship.

Meanwhile, the online shopping giant Amazon launched its own streaming service in 2014, although this differed significantly from other streaming services in that it was not solely focused on music. On the contrary, Amazon Prime – the corporation's pre-existing premium service for shoppers – added multiple new features for subscribers in the United States, the United Kingdom and Germany, including a music streaming service known as Prime Music, a video streaming service known as Prime Video, an e-book borrowing service known as the Kindle

Owners' Lending Library, and an e-book strea-ming service known as Kindle Unlimited (which is provided separately from the other premium services at an additional monthly fee). While the video and music streaming services are available for all Amazon users on a pay-per-view basis (as Amazon Video and Amazon Music), the Prime service offers subscribers access to a limited selection from its catalogue of music and videos at no extra cost, in addition to other Prime fea-tures. In 2016, Amazon also added the additional Amazon Music Unlimited subscription service, which offers users access to the site's entire mu-sic catalogue through a separate subscription. Amazon's goal is clearly not to revolutionise the market, but to attract even more users to the site so that its overall sales increase.

After purchasing YouTube in 2006 for $1.65 bil-lion, Google began pulling out all the stops to muscle in on the streaming market. As of February 2017, more than 400 hours of content are uploaded to YouTube each minute, and one billion hours of content are watched on the site every day. Furthermore, nine of the ten most-watched videos on YouTube are music videos, proving that the site is a key provider of online music. In 2014, Google launched YouTube Music Key, a music streaming service which also provided a video service. This was later rebranded as YouTube Red, a subscription service which offers users ad-free streaming of YouTube videos, and offline and background playback of videos on mobile devices. However, as of October 2017, this service remains restricted to the United States, Australia, New Zealand, Mexico and South Korea.

Tidal: the dark horse

"Our goal is simple: we want to create a better service and a better experience for both fans and artists," declared Alicia Keys at the press conference for the launch of Tidal, another competing streaming service, on 30 March 2015. None other than the rapper Jay-Z purchased this platform from the Norwegian company Aspiro at the start of 2015 for $56 million, and the site currently hosts 48.5 million songs and 175 000 music videos. The project's stated aim is to put an end to free streaming, and it counts numerous stars among its founding members: Daft Punk, Madonna, Rihanna, Coldplay, and Jack White, among others. Subscribers can choose between two services:

- the Tidal Premium service for $9.99, which offers unlimited, ad-free streaming with standard sound quality, as well as HD music videos;
- the Tidal HiFi service for $19.99, which offers unlimited, ad-free streaming with High Fidelity sound quality, as well as HD music videos.

The artist-owned site aims to give artists control over their own music and a fair share of the royalties. However, it was hit by controversy in January 2017, when the Norwegian newspaper *Dagens Næringsliv* reported that the site had been artificially inflating its user numbers. According to the article, the site had claimed to have 3 million subscribers in March 2016 (which is already a much lower number than competing sites), when the actual figure was only 850 000.

Qobuz: the niche option

Qobuz, a small French company which was founded around the same time as Deezer, provides a high-definition catalogue for the most demanding music lovers: other than Tidal, it is the only streaming service to have made its 30 million songs available in CD quality. It also provides users with a webzine featuring interviews, profiles, listening comparisons and the latest music news.

What does the future hold?

Although Spotify is still not turning a profit, with net losses of $597 million in 2016, it is still attracting investors, including the investment bank Goldman Sachs. Most recently, it raised $1 billion in financing by debt plus a discount of 20% on shares for an eventual IPO which is planned for 2018. According to analysts, streaming is seen as the future of the music industry, so it seems a foregone conclusion that, as the market leader, Spotify has a bright future ahead of it, especially given that its revenue continues to rise steadily.

Furthermore, in 2015 Spotify began integrating more diversified content, including radio, podcasts, music videos, and a selection of content from TV programmes produced by partners such as the BBC, Vice and MTV. This is a reflection of Spotify's long-term goal: by imitating the other sector giants and diversifying the site's content,

Spotify is able to offer users an even more highly personalised experience, thus attracting more users to the site and further increasing its subscriber base and presence in the sector. Assuming that the site is able to stay this course, it may even be able to increase the royalties paid to artists and thus improve its relationship with the CD industry.

SUMMARY

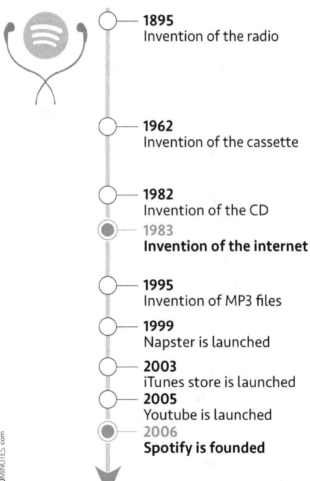

1895
Invention of the radio

1962
Invention of the cassette

1982
Invention of the CD

1983
Invention of the internet

1995
Invention of MP3 files

1999
Napster is launched

2003
iTunes store is launched

2005
Youtube is launched

2006
Spotify is founded

- Since 1999, music fans' listening habits have changed drastically due to the digitalisation of the music industry. Thanks to the advent of digital downloading (and piracy), even though listeners are generally buying less music, they are listening to it more often than ever.
- The digital revolution entered a second phase with the advent of streaming, which allowed files to be played in real time, eliminating the need to buy individual songs.
- Spotify was launched in 2008 and soon rose to become the leader in the sector. As of 2017, the site boasts 140 million active users, of whom 42% are paying subscribers, and raked in $3.3 billion in revenue in 2016.
- The site's founders aim to attract listeners who usually resort to online piracy by using a freemium model, while also creating an addiction to non-stop music consumption, whether for free or via a paid subscription.
- Despite soaring revenues, Spotify's net losses continue to increase and rose to 133% in 2016. The site has never been profitable.
- While paid music download rates are plummeting, the streaming market has fragmented: new players have burst onto the scene now

that the giants of the digital sector (Google, Apple, Amazon, etc.) have turned their attention towards the streaming market and are bringing out the big guns to entice listeners to their own platforms.

- Artists have also taken a stand: their wages took a sharp dip when paid downloads took over the market, and the royalties they receive in comparison to the volume of music listened to via streaming services are lower still. Streaming generates 22 times more revenue than the royalties received by artists.

- Streaming has also endangered the CD industry and its creators, songwriters and singers – and yet, without them, Spotify would not exist. Although the site and its competitors seem to have full confidence in their economic models, the sector must continue to evolve if it is ever to regain an equilibrium.

We want to hear from you!
Leave a comment on your online library
and share your favourite books on social media!

FURTHER READING

BIBLIOGRAPHY

- Alexander, S. (2013) Daniel Ek. *Encyclopædia Britannica*. [Online]. [Accessed 6 October 2017]. Available from: <https://www.britannica.com/biography/Daniel-Ek>

- Arnaud, C. (2000) L'Affaire Napster. *Équipe Réseaux, Savoirs & Territoires*. [Online]. [Accessed 6 October 2017]. Available from: <http://barthes.ens.fr/scpo/Presentations00-01/Arnaud_Napster/Napster.htm>

- Brunstein, J. (2014) Spotify hits 10 million paid users. Now can it make money? *Bloomberg Business*. [Online]. [Accessed 6 October 2017]. Available from: <https://www.bloomberg.com/news/articles/2014-05-21/why-spotify-and-the-streaming-music-industry-cant-make-money>

- Dauchez, A. (2011) Musique : Esquisse d'une industrie culturelle "post-piratage". *Le Monde*. [Online]. [Accessed 6 October 2017]. Available from: <http://www.lemonde.fr/idees/article/2011/03/07/musique-esquisse-d-une-industrie-culturelle-post-piratage_1488698_3232.html>

- Ek, D. (2014) $2 Billion and Counting. *Spotify*. [Online]. [Accessed 6 October 2017].

Available from: <http://news.spotify.com/us/2014/11/11/2-billion-and-counting/>

- Eveno, A. (2015) Le streaming vidéo, nouveau terrain de jeu de Spotify. *Le Monde*. [Online]. [Accessed 6 October 2017]. Available from: <http://www.lemonde.fr/economie/article/2015/05/08/le-streaming-video-nouveau-terrain-de-jeu-de-spotify_4629994_3234.html>

- Goncalves, J. (2013) Physique, téléchargement, streaming... Combien gagnent réellement les artistes ? *Charts in France*. [Online]. [Accessed 6 October 2017]. Available from: <http://www.chartsinfrance.net/actualite/news-84067.html>

- Helm, B. (2012) Inside Spotify's U.S. Invasion. *Inc*. [Online]. [Accessed 6 October 2017]. Available from: <http://www.inc.com/30under30/burt-helm/daniel-ek-founder-of-spotify.html>

- Lenoir, N. (2009) Nouvelle baisse des seuils de certification. *Purebreak Charts*. [Online]. [Accessed 6 October 2017]. Available from: <http://www.chartsinfrance.net/actualite/news-68259.html>

- Lesniak, I. (2014) Deezer, le "frenchie" qui énerve Apple, Google et Spotify. *Les Échos*. [Online]. [Accessed 6 October 2017]. Available from: <http://www.lesechos.fr/enjeux/business-stories/management/0203402250275-axel-dau-chez-en-avant-lamusique-661753.php>

- Oeillet, A. (2014) Spotify contre Taylor Swift : la rémunération des artistes en question ? *Clubic*.

[Online]. [Accessed 6 October 2017]. Available from: <http://www.clubic.com/mag/culture/actualite-738671-spotify-taylor-swift-remuneration-artistesquestion.html>

- Perelstein, L. (2013) Spotify : 4 millions de chansons n'ont jamais été écoutées. *Slate.* [Online]. [Accessed 6 October 2017]. Available from: <http://www.slate.fr/life/78902/spotify-ecoute-chansons>

- Phéline, C. (2013) Musique en ligne et partage de la valeur. État des lieux, voies de négociation et rôles de la Loi. *Culturecommunication.gouv.fr* [Online]. [Accessed 6 October 2017]. Available from: <http://culturecommunication.gouv.fr/Politiques-ministerielles/Industries-culturelles/Actualites-Archives-2013/Remise-du-rapport-de-Christian-Pheline-Musique-en-ligne-et-partage-de-la-valeur-Etat-des-lieux-voies-de-negociation-et-roles-de-la-Loi>

- Pontiroli, T. (2014) Spotify, n° 1 mondial du streaming musical, est toujours en perte. *Clubic.* [Online]. [Accessed 6 October 2017]. Available from: <http://pro.clubic.com/actualite-e-business/actualite-741399-spotify-resultats.html>

- Poussielgue, G. (2014) Musique : YouTube en guerre avec les labels indépendants. *Les Échos.* [Online]. [Accessed 6 October 2017]. Available from: <http://www.lesechos.fr/26/05/2014/LesEchos/21695-108-ECH_musique---youtube-en-guerre-avec-leslabels-independants.htm>

- Roussel, B. (2014) Le streaming confirme sa percée sur le marché américain. *Les Échos*. [Online]. [Accessed 6 October 2017]. Available from: <http://www.lesechos.fr/04/07/2014/lesechos.fr/0203619229816_le-streaming-confirme-sa-percee-sur-le-marche-americain.htm>

- Rozat, P. (2011) Deezer : la rentabilité au bout du chemin ? *InaGlobal*. [Online]. [Accessed 6 October 2017]. Available from: <http://www.inaglobal.fr/musique/article/deezer-la-rentabilite-au-bout-du-chemin>

- (No date). Spotify Press. *Spotify*. [Online]. [Accessed 6 October 2017]. Available from: <https://press.spotify.com/us/about/>

- (2014) Spotify achète la plateforme musicale intelligente The Echo Nest. *Challenges*. [Online]. [Accessed 6 October 2017]. Available from: <http://www.challenges.fr/high-tech/20140306.CHA1275/spotify-achete-la-plateforme-musicale-intelligente-the-echo-nest.html>

- (2015) Spotify a triplé ses pertes en 2014 et lorgne la vidéo en streaming. *Challenges*. [Online]. [Accessed 6 October 2017]. Available from: <http://www.challenges.fr/entreprise/20150508.CHA5659/spotify-s-apprete-a-lancer-un-service-de-video-en-streaming.html>

- (2015) Spotify lance une nouvelle fonctionnalité proposant à ses utilisateurs de nouveaux contenus multimédia (podcasts, vidéos) en plus de la musique. *Les Echos*. [Online]. [Accessed 6 October 2017]. Available from: <http://tempsreel.nouvelobs.com/en-direct/a-chaud/2354-streaming-spotify-lance-nouvelle-fonctionnalite.html>

- (2011) Spotify signe un accord de licence avec Universal Music. *Numerama*. [Online]. [Accessed 6 October 2017]. Available from: <http://www.numerama.com/magazine/19053-spotify-signe-un-accord-de-licence-avec-universal-music.html>

- Van Dievort, C. (2015) Avec TIDAL, Jay-Z part en guerre contre la musique gratuite. *La Libre Belgique*. [Online]. [Accessed 6 October 2017]. Available from: <http://www.lalibre.be/culture/musique/avec-tidal-jay-z-part-en-guerre-contre-la-musique-gratuite-551a41c83570c8b952f4a83d>

- Vion-Dury, P. (2014) Apple, Google, Deezer, Spotify... qui triomphera du streaming musical ? *L'OBS rue89*. [Online]. [Accessed 6 October 2017]. Available from: <http://rue89.nouvelobs.com/2014/07/27/apple-google-deezer-spotify-triomphera-streaming-musical-253941>

- Woitier, C. (2014) YouTube dévoile son service musical payant, Music Key. *Le Figaro*. [Online]. [Accessed 6 October 2017]. Available from: <http://www.lefigaro.fr/secteur/high-tech/2014/11/13/32001-20141113ARTFIG00185-youtube-devoile-son-service-musical-payant-music-key.php>

- Zanchi, J. (2015) La musique haute définition,

qu'est-ce que c'est exactement ? *MetroNews.*
[Online]. [Accessed 6 October 2017]. Available
from: <http://www.lci.fr/high-tech/la-musique-
haute-definition-quest-ce-que-cest-exacte-
ment-1520498.html>

ADDITIONAL SOURCES

- Guidiri, M. (2015) *Freemium.* Trans. Probert, C.
  Brussels: Plurilingua Publishing.

- IFPI website: <http://www.ifpi.org/>

- Qobuz website: <http://www.qobuz.com>

- Spotify website: <https://www.spotify.com/>

- Tradedoubler website: <http://www.tradedoubler.
  com/en/>

www.50minutes.com

Ebook EAN: 9782808002387

Paperback EAN: 9782808002394

Legal Deposit: D/2017/12603/640

Cover: © Primento

Digital conception by Primento, the digital partner of publishers.

Printed in the USA
CPSIA information can be obtained
at www.ICGtesting.com
LVHW011509251123
764902LV00068B/4473